CRYSTAL SKULL
CONSCIOUSNESS

Shelley Kaehr, Ph.D.

CRYSTAL SKULL CONSCIOUSNESS

Shelley Kaehr, Ph.D.

FIRST EDITION
First Printing, 2007

Edited by Linnea M Armstrong

Library of Congress Control Number: 2007920537
Kaehr, Shelley A., 1967—
          Crystal Skull Consciousness/
Shelley Kaehr — 1st ed.
p.   cm.
Includes bibliographical references.
ISBN: 978-0-9648209-4-4

An Out of This World Production does not have any authority concerning private business transactions between our authors and the public. If you wish to contact the author or would like more information about this book, please write to the author in care of An Out of This World Production and we will forward your request. Please write to:

Shelley Kaehr, Ph.D.
c/o An Out of This World Production
P.O. Box 610943
Dallas, TX 75261-0943

"Conventional opinion is the
ruin of our souls."

—Rumi

ACKNOWLEDGEMENTS

Thank You to the following individuals without whom this project could not have happened:

Joy and Larry Kauf – for messages of joy

Linnea M. Armstrong – for your calming presence in my life

Jane Li Fox – for your ever-supportive friendship

My family – Mickey, Gail and Mark – for being there

I THANK YOU ALL!

CONTENTS

SKULLS AS SYMBOLS

Introduction

In the past two years, I have been exposed to what I think must be a growing craze amongst the population: an obsession with skulls that I choose to call *Skull Consciousness*.

Although this book will focus on the crystal versions, which are the subject of much mysterious controversy and modern-day folklore, I'll take a look at the concept of skulls in general, as they seem to be the focus of a cultural phenomenon gaining more and more momentum lately.

When I talked to friends about this book project, which I've been contemplating for the past several months, many of them had never even heard of it before; others seemed to have been in on it for years. It just goes to show—you never really know your own friends!

The purpose of *Crystal Skull Consciousness* is to discuss the skulls, their origins and how they may be used in healing, with the hope that you may become aware and maybe even interested in this yourself.

The skulls have long been associated with a very deep part of ourselves. My hope is that through them you may, as I have, come to a greater understanding of yourself and reason for being.

Obsession with the Human Form

I recently visited the controversial "Body Worlds," Gunther von Hagens' controversial exhibition of real human bodies.

For those who have not yet heard of this, the exhibit includes five full galleries of plasticized human bodies, displayed with the intent of showing viewers the functions of our innermost workings.

I first heard of this morbid display while I was in New York City last fall, and everyone there was buzzing about it. When I heard it was coming to Dallas, I wanted to see it. Why, I cannot explain; just curious, I guess. I waited until the tour was almost over and something told me it would be beneficial to see it.

At this writing, I can say I am glad I did. What I saw there illustrated an excellent example of what I will be talking about in this book.

It seems we human beings have a fascination with our own form. Whether we're staring at fashion magazines, studying "muscle beach" body builders, or looking at dead bodies, we have a genetically programmed, cultural obsession with ourselves, so to speak. This concept was so clearly evident while I went through "Body Worlds" that I wanted to bring it to your attention, so you would also be aware of this on a more conscious level.

First, this exhibit was not as grotesque as I thought it would be. (Originally, I wanted to go on an empty stomach lest I have the urge to toss my cookies!) I was surprised, though, to find that the people on display did not seem real to me. Yes, they still had certain unique characteristics, particularly in their faces. But that unknowable part of them that I so often mention in my other books—their souls—were clearly gone, therefore making them not as real.

One of the most interesting things about the exhibit was that you could actually look inside others, and see where your own organs are, therebye understanding yourself on a deeper level. It brought that boring high school biology class to life in a way few things could! I looked very closely at everything there was to see there!

But something happened at one point during the exhibit that I found extremely illuminating: as I stared wide-eyed at one of the displays, I realized I was unconsciously pointing to my own torso and looking at the location of the corresponding part of my own body. I happened to glance at a child standing next to me and saw him doing the same thing!

This led me to take a broader look around the room. I quickly noticed that several people in the packed gallery were engaging in the same activity.

When I left, I felt I had a much deeper understanding of my own inner workings. When I spoke with the friend who went with me a couple of days later, he said, "It's weird, but now when I see people, I feel like I can look right through them and know exactly what they look like under their skin." I felt the same way. This certainly brings a new dimension to the notion of "undressing people with your eyes"!

This brings me back to the skulls. Our fascination with skulls—crystal or otherwise—is part of our collective consciousness, and part of not only our culture, but of humanity at large.

There is an old saying that the machine can never understand itself. It's something I bring up often in my lectures when people come up to ask me what I think of the soul and where we're going when we die. I tell them the same thing I will tell you here: I cannot know the mind of God, and never will be able to, simply because we are all merely mortal. Although we all can (and do) have a wide variety of feelings and opinions about how the universe works, we will never, in my opinion, know for certain what our creator has in store for us until we are gone.

As "the machine," I must say "Body Worlds" gave me what I now consider to be the closest look at myself I can ever remember having.

CRYSTAL SKULL CONSCIOUSNESS

Aside from these types of exhibits, I think the best way to understand ourselves is history, particularly the study of those who have gone before us.

When we look into the world of skull consciousness, we can clearly see that the obsession with the human form is no new phenomenon. It has been going on since the beginnings of time throughout indigenous cultures all over the world.

We will explore some of these things in the book, and also discuss the common myths and legends surrounding the most famous crystal skulls in history. Some believe these skulls have mystical, supernatural, or even extraterrestrial origins. Regardless of where they came from, they are clearly important phenomena that it merit us taking a closer look at as we strive to understand ourselves at a deeper level.

Let's begin our journey into the world of Crystal Skulls!

The Thirteen

One of the most baffling subjects in modern archeology is the discovery of thirteen skulls of supposed ancient origin found in the areas around Mexico, Central and South America—the regions of the ancient Maya and Aztec civilizations.

Nobody is certain where or when these skulls were created, but some speculation suggests they may be between 5,000 and 36,000 years old. Their discovery rivals other modern mysteries such as the Great Pyramids at Giza, the Peruvian Nazca Lines, or Stonehenge.

Indigenous peoples from throughout these regions have claimed for years that the skulls have magical healing properties.

"Be occupied, then, with
what you really value and let
the thief take something else."

—Rumi

ORIGINS OF
CRYSTAL SKULLS

"Patience is the key to joy."

—Rumi

Shelley Kaehr, Ph.D.

Atlantis

Nobody knows with certainty the crystal skulls' origins. Skeptics say they're merely fakes, while others claim they are the keys to lost worlds and times long past.

Some mystics suggest the skulls may have originated in the Lemurian or Atlantean civilizations originally described by psychic Edgar Cayce. I first became interested in working on this project through my research for the book, *Edgar Cayce's Guide to Gemstones, Minerals, Metals & More* (ARE Press, 2005). Cayce said so much about so many things that have given us clues to our own origins and our ultimate destiny that the Work, as he called it, continues to baffle scholars to this day.

Cayce was one of the first in recent history to discuss and describe in great detail the civilization of Atlantis and the one that came before it, Lemuria. Although there is no mention of the skulls in the Work, he most definitely described crystals used in these ancient times by the people who lived then.

Atlantean legends tell us the people there were extremely versed in all things crystalline, and past life regression reports I've received from clients supports this. It is possible that the skulls were around then, but I am inclined to think they originate from an even earlier time in ancient Lemuria.

Lemuria

I wrote a book a while back about the special crystals that are now being discovered that have ties to the lost continent of Lemuria, called *Lemurian Seeds: Hope for Humanity*.

After much research on this phenomenon, it is believed that the crystals were planted millions of years ago like tiny seeds that have now grown up and are being discovered all over the world.

I reported in that book that although they were only being found in Brazil and Russia, that soon these special stones would start turning up all around the world. I can now report that since that writing, I have met mine operators of Seed Crystal mines from India, seen the seeds on my travels through Nepal, and heard of people who have seen them in Australia, New Zealand and other sites around the globe. It seems that they really are being discovered everywhere.

The concept of the seed crystals and their telepathic link to peaceful energies and the shifting of consciousness is similar to the skull phenomenon.

Atlantis or Lemuria?

The Atlantean civilization has historically been perceived as possessing very male-dominated energy. Certainly, the skull shape tends to take on that masculine energy as well.

Lemuria represents the more feminine, receptive side of our nature. The civilization seems energetically to be far more primitive, also reminiscent of the skulls.

So if these artifacts somehow have links to these most ancient of times, which place did they come from?

Of course we can never know for sure, but I am inclined to think they originated in Lemuria and were carried over to the healing temples of Atlantis.

During the great shift of that time, Lemurians made their way across land bridges into the regions of Atlantis and perhaps, for a few generations, had a great deal of influence on the early Atlantean civilization.

In our own culture today, we can see how our grandparents influenced us to a certain degree. With younger people, however, we notice how they seem more removed from us and our current values. This is particularly evident with the influx of the Indigo Children, the new children with bluish auras who have been called "super psychics."

Similarly, in ancient times, I am sure the influence of Lemuria was felt more powerfully in the beginning. Once a few generations passed, the old ways started to die off and the more masculine energies began to take over, almost in rebellion against the old ways.

While skulls may have been present in the earlier healing temples of Atlantis, they may have come to be seen as symbols of the old outmoded ways and subsequently disregarded. The skulls—representing the image of man, truth and dignity—were disregarded as envy, greed and power began to take over the hearts and minds of the Atlanteans.

Are the skull forms emerging more frequently today as a gentle reminder of times past, urging us to take the higher road and more peaceful ways? We can only speculate.

Shelley Kaehr, Ph.D.

EXTRATERRESTRIALS

Some people—myself among them—believe these thirteen skulls are linked to each other telepathically and could possibly be communication tools through which we receive energy and information from other worlds, whether that world is an ancient earthly society or someplace even farther away.

The skulls certainly could have originated from a higher intelligence in a distant galaxy and are being used to transmit messages and energies to us here on earth.

There is a school of thought that says the Lemurians themselves were not regular beings in physical form, as we think about people today; rather, they were more multi-dimensional in nature and that they are still among us, often living underground in such spiritual hot spots as Mount Shasta, California.

It's possible that these beings are so advanced they are able to shift realities with a mere thought and travel light years between our world, times past, and completely different universes in mere seconds.

CRYSTAL SKULL CONSCIOUSNESS

There are so many mysteries in the world that defy all logic, and it is certainly possible that those things that fall into the realm of the unexplained—such as the Great Pyramids, Stonehenge, and even the crystal skulls—are all products of the same otherworldly and super intelligent force.

Particularly when you take a look at all the unbelievable technological advances we've been making, particularly over the past fifty years, I'm sure I don't have to tell you that there is truly no logical explanation for some of these phenomena.

My parents talk about times when they did not have televisions. *Their* parents talk about times with no indoor plumbing.

In the grand scheme of geological history, the number of years ago that people were living under such circumstances doesn't add up to the blink of an eye. Look at us now! We are rivaling George Jetson and will most likely soon surpass him!

It is not too far-fetched to think that other-worldly intelligence is communicating with us all through a variety of means—perhaps even through crystal skulls.

Of course, nobody knows this for sure, but if we in modern times are able to transmit millions of pieces of data to each other through our crystalline computer chips, would it not make sense that an otherworldly civilization could be transmitting information to us through crystals of all kinds, particularly those of skull shape since they provide an outer reflection of our own inner workings?

It's certainly interesting to think about!

"Brother stand the pain; Escape the poison of your impulses. The sky will bow to your beauty, if you do. Learn to light the candle. Rise with the sun. Turn away from the cave of your sleeping. That way a thorn expands to a rose. A particular glows with the universal."

—Rumi

Shelley Kaehr, Ph.D.

Mayan

There are numerous theories which suggest the skulls originated in the Mayan civilization, particularly since one of the most famous skulls was said to have been gifted from Mayan elders, yet this theory has not held up simply because the skull image is not prevalent in Mayan culture.

You can notice by either visiting or looking at photos of ruins at Palenque, Copan or Tikal that the skull form is nowhere to be found.

Images and drawings have more rounded features and do not seem consistent with the skulls found in other ruins.

"Everything in the universe
is a pitcher brimming with
wisdom and beauty."

—Rumi

Aztecs

It is more likely that if the skulls are indeed ancient that they originated from the Aztecs, who have many skull images in their architecture.

On a trip to Chitzen-Itza, the pyramids near Cancun and Cozumel, I noticed skull forms in the brick there to commemorate the fallen and those who succumbed to plague.

"Burdens are the foundations of ease and bitter things the forerunners of pleasure."

—Rumi

FAMOUS SKULLS

"Don't allow your animal nature to rule your reason."

—Rumi

MITCHELL-HEDGES CRYSTAL SKULL

This skull is probably the most famous—and controversial—of all the skulls in existence.

It was supposedly discovered in 1927 in Lubaantun in British Honduras by Anna Mitchell-Hedges, adopted daughter of famed explorer F.A. Mitchell-Hedges.

F.A. Mitchell-Hedges was leading an expedition into what is now modern-day Belize to locate evidence of the lost continent of Atlantis when Anna found the skull inside an old temple ruin.

When she discovered the skull, it was missing its jawbone, which was found only 25 feet away a month later. Mitchell-Hedges allegedly offered the skull back to the Mayan priests, who gave it to him as a gift upon his departure.

This fantastical story has been said to be a complete fabrication, since evidence now suggests Mitchell-Hedges purchased the piece at a 1943 auction in Sotheby's in London. The British Museum, which bid against Mitchell-Hedges, has documents proving this allegation.

It is also interesting to note that no photos were taken of the skull prior to 1943, nor did Mitchell-Hedges even acknowledge its existence before that time.

Regardless of this controversy, the skull underwent extensive tests by Hewlett-Packard in the 1970s, after which the lab concluded that the skull was carved completely against the grain—which no modern sculptor would do—and that there were no markings on it to suggest it had been carved either by hand or by machine.

The construction of the skull, therefore, was deemed none other than miraculous. For that reason, it is considered a true wonder of the world.

Skull of Doom

The Mitchell-Hedges skull is sometimes referred to as the 'skull of doom,' because it was said to command forces that would kill enemies in battle in the Mayan culture.

Skeptics assert this foreboding tale was fabricated by Mitchell-Hedges, yet it is reminiscent of documented cases of Kahuna warfare in Hawaii.

Shelley Kaehr, Ph.D.

THERE ARE STILL BELIEVERS!

I had the opportunity to meet a wonderful new friend on one of my annual Tucson pilgrimages and spent quite a bit of time talking to him. He happens to be a personal friend of Anna Mitchell-Hedges and spent a long time himself in deep meditation and contemplation with this particular skull and believes without a doubt that the skull is not only authentic, but of great spiritual and universal importance.

"He is a letter to everyone.
You open it. It says, 'Live!'"

—Rumi

Shelley Kaehr, Ph.D.

BRITISH & PARIS CRYSTAL SKULLS

Two of the other most famous skulls now reside in the Museums of Man in both London and Paris and were supposedly bought by mercenaries in Mexico in the 1890's.

I had the opportunity to visit London last year and went to the British Museum to see the skull that has been housed there since 1898.

A placard under the skull says:

Rock Crystal Skull

Late 19th c AD

It was originally thought to be Aztec but recent research proves it to be European.

Purchased from Tiffany & Co. NY through Mr. GF Kunz Ethno 1898-1

GF Kunz was the famous gemologist who worked for Tiffany's, who wrote the incredible book called *The Curious Lore of Precious Stones.*

Regardless of the authenticity of the British Skull, I cannot dispute the incredible energy that emitted from it; I could feel it from across the room. In fact, it dwarfed all the other amazing artifacts in the place.

I got as close to it as I could and studied it carefully for a few minutes. Then I went and sat down and just watched as other people observed it. Many seemed to have the same reaction to it as I had. It draws people to it through its immense energy.

Later in the book in the skull transmissions section, I will describe in detail the notes I took while contemplating the British skull.

I have written so much about the power of stones themselves, yet these pieces seem to have an added power, if you will, of being carved in the shape of the skull. It's as if they are somehow able to tap into the hologram of our own physical form now and through all time. It is truly incredible!

MAX — THE TEXAN

One of the other most famous skulls in existence today is alleged to be of Guatemalan origin and was passed into the hands of Jo Ann Parks of Houston, Texas.

I happened to see Max years ago at a sort of "cocktail social viewing."

It was my very first introduction to the idea of crystal skulls and what they are.

Of all the skulls I know of, I have a particular affinity for dear Max. He has a wonderful energy to him! He's also close to home for me and seems like an old friend.

In fact, I credit Max with opening up the awareness of skull consciousness in the U.S. Thanks both to his accessibility and to the generosity of his keeper, Jo Ann, thousands of people, including yours truly, are now aware of the crystal skull phenomenon!

Up-and-Coming Skull: Clyde, Lewisville, Texas

How I Fell In Love With Clyde

Clyde is a wonderful skull owned by my friends Joy and Larry at a shop called Messages of Joy in Texas. He is featured on the cover of the book and has a wonderful energy about him.

We originally met when I was in the shop one day. I noticed him, but he didn't say much to me at first.

Occasionally, I would wonder about him and whether he was still there; then something interesting happened.

One night I was at home eating my dinner when I had a feeling I needed to walk over to the shop to get some skulls who wanted to be photographed for this book, including Clyde.

I wasn't sure the store would even be open since it was getting late, but I had an urgent feeling I needed to go immediately, so I did. Larry was there when I walked in. I asked him if I could take home some of the skulls and he agreed to let me work with them.

I raced back to my house with the three you see pictured here, and began to photograph them immediately. I was surprised at how willing they were to be photographed. I may not have mentioned this in my other gem books, but the stones are sometimes quite funny about being photographed. I don't know if they carry a preconceived notion of what it would mean to have their picture taken, but all I can say is that sometimes the gem photography projects can be quite time consuming.

You may have heard of the Native American belief that when someone takes your picture they can take a bit of your soul, and I wonder if some stones feel that way too. The point is, that when they are so amenable to being photographed, it makes me realize it is truly meant to be.

The only other time I can remember stones wanting to be pictured as much as these skulls was when I did the photography for my book, *Lemurian Seeds: Hope for Humanity.* Those seed crystals were also anxious to be in a book. Maybe it is because the Lemurian energies are so prevalent right now. Since I think the skulls have some of that energy, it makes sense that they are urgently calling to be seen at this time. It is quite remarkable!

When I brought the three skulls home and took their photos, I realized that the clear quartz one really wanted to be photographed alone. He had a powerful energy about him and I realized I was in the presence of a truly incredible being of some kind. I began to sense he had something to say.

"What is your name?" I asked.

"Clyde," he answered, clear as a bell.

At first, I was surprised that he had such a strong presence about him. It was clear that there was a very special being within this skull form who seemed to have encompassed the wisdom and knowledge of all the other skulls I had ever seen. I decided to take advantage of his information and asked him more.

"What are the skulls about on an energetic level?" I asked.

"They are an outer reflection of consciousness and as people work with the image of themselves, they can learn to explore their own inner consciousness at a deeper level."

"Where are the skulls from?"

"They were originally from a galaxy far from here, in the outer regions of the universe, although it is hard to describe it as a galaxy because I do not think you on earth can understand what the universe is really like. It is beyond your understanding when you are in physical form."

"How can you assist us?" I asked.

"When you work with us, just be open to receive divine communication from other realms and know that we will assist you in tapping into ideas from all beings who have come before you and who are yet to incarnate," Clyde said.

Since meditating with Clyde I can say that I have felt a deep sense of peace and grounding I have not quite experienced before.

More on that in the section on healing, but for now, I can say it is a powerful love affair I have going – with a crystal skull!

After this experience, I took Clyde back to Larry and Joy and now other people have started to visit Clyde and meditate with him and have had some interesting experiences with him. He is one of my personal favorite skulls that I have ever seen!

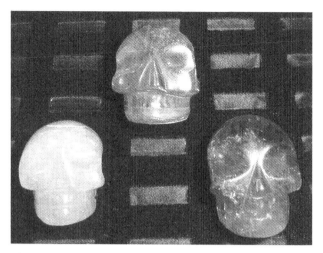

The three crystal skulls from Messages of Joy in Lewisville, TX. Clyde (center) is composed of clear quartz. The skull on the left is rose quartz; the right skull is made of amethyst.

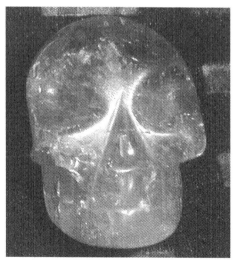

A closeup of the amethyst skull.

"If you are irritated by every rub, how will you be polished?"

—Rumi

HOW TO COMMUNICATE
WITH THE SKULLS

Speaking of communing with skulls, there are several ways you can receive information with them.

The first and best way would be through meditation while in the presence of the skull. If it is one of the famous ones and it is behind glass, you can simply sit near it and begin to tune into it by speaking to it in your mind and asking it what it would like to tell you or what you need to know at the present time.

The advantage of skulls like Clyde is that you can actually go to the shop and see him and sit with him in your hands, which would be yet another way to commune with the skull. Clyde is still a bit more accessible than some of the others, which is great! It may not always be that way, but at least for now, he is there and available!

As I have said in other books, though, it is never necessary to be in physical presence of anything to tap into its wisdom or its energy. In quantum physics, for example, it is said that the further you are from a particular object the more powerful it can be which is why energy healing or prayer work. More on that in a bit, but suffice it to say that the skull you want to talk to can be accessed through your mind's eye, your imagination, or whatever you want to call that more intuitive side of your nature, simply by asking to go there!

As with any kind of spiritual experience, you need to do what feels right for you!

HEALING USES
OF SKULLS

"I am burning. If anyone lacks tinder, let him set his rubbish ablaze with my fire."

—Rumi

Shelley Kaehr, Ph.D.

Psychic Power

Some believe the skulls of the ancients have incredible healing powers. There are legends that suggest indigenous peoples actually store the skulls in safekeeping under the tight lock and key of guards and tribal elders who secure their safety. Why? Because they have incredible powers to heal the sick and infirm and give energy and power to those who come in contact with them.

Modern-day skull philosophy involves using the form of the skull to tap into the holographic impression of all those who came before and therefore tap into those healing powers.

Setting intention on what you want to create when working with your skull, is of paramount importance.

Do you want to increase your psychic abilities? The skull image is a strong symbol for that.

Exercise for Third Eye Opening

While holding your own crystal skull, close your eyes and concentrate on the area around your forehead. Imagine you can feel the energy of your third eye opening to receive the wisdom of the ages.

Ask that a purple beam of light move down through the top of your head and into your forehead while you concentrate on this opening.

Exercise to open yourself to Times Long Ago

While doing the previous exercise, you can also try the following:

Ask to be shown all you need to know at this time and allow yourself to be open to all the pictures, thoughts and feelings that come to you.

If you'd like, ask the skull to show you things of times past, and notice what you see and feel.

Do this process as often as you'd like and experiment to see what occurs to you, depending on what kinds of information you request. It is fun to practice!

Physical Healing

You can also use skulls in healing when dealing with someone suffering from ailments involving the head.

This could include anything from physical conditions such as migraines or allergies, to mental conditions such as hyperactivity or depression. (Of course, if you have a serious physical or mental condition, you should always seek the help of a qualified professional.)

It could also be used to rectify a difficult state of mind, or to clear one's mind to get the highest and best solution to a problem.

Clear your crystal skull by either putting it outside in the sun, moon or rain, by cleansing it in sea salt water, by activating and clearing it with Reiki, or by using the clearing stone, Selenite.

Once the stone is clear, infuse it with the energies of the person for whom you are doing the healing. The person could be in the room, but more likely they are not. You would use the skull form to symbolize their physical embodiment.

CRYSTAL SKULL CONSCIOUSNESS

Visualize the person receiving the healing and imagine light pouring from your hands, into both the skull and the person you're trying to help. Imagine the person is in a state of total peace and perfection and that whatever you are sending them will be fully received.

If you are adding energy, imagine they received it.

If something needs to be removed, imagine the light you are sending through your hands is easily displacing the unwanted influences and putting high frequency light in its place.

Continue this process as long as your hands are warm and you are guided to do so.

SELF HEALING

If you're the one needing the healing, follow the same steps listed in the previous section with one difference: put your hands on the skull and imagine you are allowing it to amplify and rectify the energies within you, giving you a cosmic "kick-start."

Imagine that whatever unwanted conditions have are gone; imagine that you already have whatever you would like to have.

You can direct the skull consciously to do what you ask. I have found to be even more powerful is to simply ask the skull to assist you with whatever kind of healing is needed for your highest good at this time.

That way you are giving permission for any situation which may exist outside your conscious awareness to be remedied.

We do this, usually, when we are offering healing to other people. However, when it comes to working on ourselves, we cannot always see ourselves clearly. We often assume we know exactly what is happening with us when many times, we don't.

CRYSTAL SKULL CONSCIOUSNESS

When I teach group healing classes and we work on others, our prayer is always that we are allowing whatever healing needs to occur to happen for their highest and best; for ourselves, though, this is tough to do. We are often too busy thinking of others to remember that we must care for ourselves first before we can offer anything to anyone else. That's a powerful lesson, one I think most of us are still working on!

So back to the subject of healing yourself, here are the steps once again:

1) Placing your hands on the skull, close your eyes.

2) Ask the skull to assist you at this time with healing anything that is for highest and best.

3) Notice your hands may start to get hot and just allow the flow of energy to move through you without judgement

4) Continue the healing on yourself as long as you are guided, or until the hands cool down and you feel like opening your eyes.

Try this! Working with the skulls is powerful!

Shelley Kaehr, Ph.D.

SKRYING —
ANCIENT ART OF DIVINATION

The other way you can use the skulls for healing and information is to engage in the age old practice of scrying, or gazing.

Normally this is done with a regular crystal ball, but the skulls are wonderful tools to use as well.

You can use any kind of stone skull you'd like, but the crystal variety may work best. Here are the steps you need to do this:

1) Get a dark piece of cloth
2) Sit in a semi-darkened room
3) Put the crystal skull in your lap
4) Drape the dark or black cloth over your head
5) Stare down into the skull with your eyes defocused
6) Allow yourself to simply stare without judgment and see if you can notice any images or visions emanating from the skull
7) Continue until your eyes are tired or the pictures stop

One thing to keep in mind when you do this is that the room needs to be darkened but not completely dark, because the skull is illuminated to a certain degree by the light coming in. It won't work if there's too much light, but if it's too dark, you won't be able to see anything either.

This same process can be done using any crystal ball, be it natural or man-made, or with mirrors.

I've talked in other books about staring into a mirror. Normally what shows up when you defocus your eyes are images of who you used to be in previous lives. It is really interesting to experiment with this stuff!

The best way I can describe what I am talking about when I say "defocus your eyes," is to do what you do when you are staring at those dot cartoons in the Sunday newspaper where they ask you to notice what picture you see within the dots.

For years I could not do this and then one day I just finally figured it out! You hold the paper really close to your eyes and somehow look beyond the paper and go past where it is as if it was not there. After a couple minutes of simple staring a 3-D image suddenly begins to pop out/ As you slowly pull the paper away from your eyes, the entire 3-D image becomes crystal clear.

Skrying into crystal balls or skulls is similar.

You'll be sitting there not seeing a thing, when suddenly, you'll likely to see a little movie running in it. It's truly amazing!

What I find interesting about the skulls is that the information you see there is usually of a different quality than that of what you'll see in a plain crystal. Often, you can actually see the images of those past times you are wondering about. These visions make me believe that the skulls are some true form of consciousness that we can tap into for the betterment of us all.

"Looking up gives light, although at first it makes you dizzy."

—Rumi

Skull Transmissions

As I mentioned earlier in the book, I took a trip to the British Museum in London, where I had the opportunity to sit for quite some time with the skull there. I received a complete outpouring of information that I wrote in my journal, and that wish to share with you now.

First, I asked about the Mitchell-Hedges skull and its meaning and origins:

The Mitchell- Hedges skull tells me it is tired of all the scandal surrounding its origins and that it is both Aztec and a gift for Mitchell-Hedges' daughter.

He was offered to Mr. Mitchell-Hedges by a mysterious tradesman. He purchased it for pennies and then hid it for his daughter's birthday.

Then, I inquired about the British Skull:

The interior lines in the stone look wispy and follow the same lines as the veins in our head.

This being is Pleiadian in origin and has been on earth for 25 million years as a cornerstone of a great grid.

Initially, these were placed in particular parts of the jungle for a reason, and they were never meant to be removed from their spots. But of course, the greediness of man crept in and this skull was displaced.

Now it is in the British Museum and it has reconfigured itself so that all is well once again. It would be like rebooting a computer with a new software program. Once it was removed, it just rebooted itself and can now do its work from here.

There are over 500 skulls still buried under-ground in key locations around the globe that are never meant to be found.

The ones that have been discovered were allowed to be because the skull consciousness agreed that in order to make a deeper impact on our subconscious, it would help if people could find a few of them and those, in turn, could com-municate through the still-hidden grid buried beneath the earth like a networked phone sys-tem. There, they are all linked with each other no matter where on earth they are.

What is the significance of skull carvings and why are they important to us now...or are they?

When man chooses to carve crystal in skull form, it is because skull consciousness is de-manding it be done as further means of convey-ing its higher purpose, messages and energies.

So it is invalid to say that even the tiniest skull is not significant. They are all linked to-

gether through the hologram of the universe.

In your world, you have phone power boxes, telephones and cell phones, each being removed from their source and central thoughtform; yet, none are insignificant.

What are the skulls about?

1) Compassion

2) Connection – you are needing help in this area, which is why they show up

3) Humanity – a visual representation of the form of man to remind you to think of each other and not levy destructive forces on mankind. In order to keep yourselves in physical form, you need to honor and respect that form, which is represented by skulls

4) Human Condition – located in a gallery with walls, talking about human suffering, is designed to help us help each other

5) Love

As I write this, I am reminded to tell you about the gallery in the British Museum where the skull is located, as item #4 suggests.

The placard on that section of the exhibition says:

"People everywhere experience trouble, sorrow, need and sickness and develop skills and

knowledge in response to these adversities."

Interestingly, this is something I often talk about in lectures: the fact that we humans tend to learn through pain rather than through pleasure. It is the collective "way of the old" I think we are doing our best to change, but change is often slow.

I write these books so I can help others learn without going through immense suffering. I work with clients with that same goal in mind. All we have to do is change the way we react to the world and soon, everything begins to change. It is that bad things are happening to us – those things will happen. It is our response to those things that matters and and learning to choose peace over war.

I recently had a situation arise in my own life which initially I believed could escalate into a legal matter. I went ahead and ran through all the scenarios in my mind of how this could play out legally and wrote the people involved letters I never sent. Afterwards, I instantly felt better about things and went to sleep.

The next day, a floodgate of new information washed over me. I realized there was a whole new way of handling things without any kind of confrontation. I chose to basically ignore the problem and imagine that it was not a problem at all. As a result, things instantly became better.

The law of attraction was at work again! I think we are all running unconscious programs of the past as far as how we deal with stress and react to things in our lives.

If we could all go ahead and do what we want off the cuff and on paper only, play things out in our minds, then give ourselves a day or two to let things sink in before taking any kind of action in the physical plane, wars and conflicts of all kinds may be avoided entirely.

I believe the skulls are here to remind us both of this fact and to take care of our physical form as part of the universe at large. It is an important and timely message.

"No mirror ever
became iron again;
No bread ever
became wheat;
No ripened grape ever
became sour fruit.
Mature yourself and be
secure from a change
for the worse.
Become the light."

—Rumi

Shelley Kaehr, Ph.D.

THE SKULL FROM MOUNT SHASTA

The following section is an excerpt from my earlier book, *Lemurian Seeds: Hope for Humanity*, in which I first gained the understanding that at least some of the crystal skulls originated from ancient Lemuria:

I met some people at a show in Memphis who offered to let me commune with one of their crystal skulls. They had a table with about a dozen skulls of all sizes and all kinds of material from fluorite to amber to hematite.

I scanned them with my hand to see which ones I felt the most energy around and without a doubt, the strongest one was a smaller sample made of lava rock from none other than Mount Shasta.

I held it in my right hand, scanned it with my left hand and the store owner sent me some energy through my crown. Almost instantly, I saw Shasta in my mind's eye and felt the energy of the skull.

I felt it had connections to the ancient Lemurians and saw visions of the lemurs. I could see how the size of this skull could compare to that of a modern-day lemur.

CRYSTAL SKULL CONSCIOUSNESS

I had a vision of the seed crystals in Brazil, then in Russia, poking up from the ground. Then my vision expanded to the entire world, and I began to see lights all over the world, representing all the places where the Lemurian seed crystals actually existed, though nobody had found them yet. These places included Australia, New Zealand, Polynesia, Tibet, other parts of South America, India, and Africa.

When I scanned Africa, I went up toward Egypt and saw there are none in the desert there but they are under the Nile. lining it. I also saw the seed crystals under the Tigris and Euphrates in what used to be Mesopotamia (now modern-day Turkey). The seed crystals are lining these areas to hold the consciousness of these sacred spots as the seeds of our current civilization.

Then I found myself at the Sphinx and went inside. Under the ground, I saw a tunnel that fell like a mine shaft deep in the earth. It reminded me of being on a roller coaster in an amusement park, particularly Space Mountain at Disney-land, if you have ever ridden that deep space ride where you cannot see a foot in front of you. The narrow tube fell straight down into the earth, and I actually felt the sensation of falling, as if on a roller coaster. At times, it would level off or make a turn, then drop farther down. It was strange, to say the least. It was so real I could not recall that I was actually still sitting in the room at the show.

At this point, I took a deep gulp of air, came up, and opened my eyes for a split second. When I saw I was in the room, I closed them again and started up top. I went through the tunnels again, only this time much faster, and kept continuously falling until I finally landed on the bottom in a cavern with the most amazing huge crystals I had ever seen.

They had giant keys on them like their smaller counterparts as well as the horizontal striations, but instead of rubbing your hand over these, you could lean against them. Layer by layer, each line would reveal different information and lit up my whole being.

It was unreal. I felt so energized! Although I do not consciously know what happened with that, I felt I received an initiation of some kind, a "download" that will benefit me for the rest of my life.

Just as with the smaller versions, these striations contain data, and you are like a computer uploading this stuff. But in the giant crystal cavern, it was like going to the motherboard of the whole operation and becoming one with it all. It was one of the profound experiences I have ever had.

I stood next to these crystals that were taller than most buildings you see. The temperature around my body began to decrease as I felt the high frequency of these amazing giant Lemurian Seeds.

The feeling I had there in the center of the earth was that of a profound grounding the likes of which I had never felt.

I knew I was in "command central" for the Lemurian Seed crystals, where the very first ones were planted. Just like a tree growing for thousands of years, these crystals had been there millions, even billions of years, growing to unbelievable heights.

The earth lit up again from the outside and I could once more see how these original pieces and the other tiny fragments planted not just in Brazil, but all over the earth, were holding a particular frequency grid for the whole planet. It was pretty cosmic!

Have you seen those potatoes when they stick cloves in them or one of those plastic dog toys with the pointy spikes stick in and out all over it? That is what this looked like.

These interdimensional beings created a vast network that we are only now just begin-ning to tap into. Over many years to come, more of these amazing specimens are going to be discovered by the folks who need them most. Meanwhile, they are fine where they are because they are serving purpose by just being there. The higher purpose is going to unfold as our con-

sciousness allows us to notice more and more of them and activate other keys of consciousness to reshape our destiny.

When the woman gently patted my shoulders and told me my session was over, I was already right there with her. I had come up from the depths of the core of earth and when I opened my eyes and stood up, the soles of my feet were deeply connected to our earth like I had never experienced before, in this life anyway.

It was an awesome experience! I am grateful for the opportunity to work with the Lemurian skull.

Now that I've had more time to work with both the Lemurian Seed Crystals and the Crystal Skulls, I am more convinced than ever that the purpose for both tools is very similar: to bring hope and healing to humanity and to lend a peaceful vibration to Mother Earth.

"No prayer is complete
without presence."

—Rumi

SKULLS AS SYMBOLS

"Paradise is surrounded by what we dislike; the fires of hell are surrounded by what we desire."

—Rumi

Skull Symbology

As a symbol, skulls are powerful links to the past, present and future of man and seem to show up in just about every culture on earth, symbolizing everything from mortality and death to initiation and empowerment.

Often in ancient ceremonial sites around the globe, skull figures or carvings etched in stone represent the numbers of those who perished in war or times of famine.

On a more modern note, a friend called just the other day to tell me about observing her friend's daughter in the shopping mall, and how the skull phenomenon is really big right now in kids' clothing. It doesn't surprise me.

We also saw the marketing at work as the Disney Corporation released the *Pirates of the Caribbean* series. Everyone wanted their own skull and crossbones T-shirt to commemorate the film. Disney once again proves their marketing genius!

Take a look around and I'm sure you'll see skull consciousness is abundant in our world.

A recent issue of fashion magazine *Elle* featured a whole section devoted to the stone skull carvings in jewelry. Let's face it, if the fashion industry is catching on to skulls, it means this craze is really taking off!

Skull Consciousness in Modern Times

There are several famous skulls located in different parts of the world and owned by collectors, none of which can be authentically linked to ancient times.

But does this really matter?

The skulls described in this book are both modern and potentially ancient in origin. Many people, including myself, believe these skulls are energetically linked to the ancients and to other worlds as well, as if just creating the intention in physical form of a skull somehow links humankind to all the skulls that have come before.

If the message of these skulls truly is one of peace and compassion for fellow human beings, it is wonderful that skulls are infiltrating our collective consciousness at this time. We can only hope they, along with other metaphysical tools, are able to assist us all at this time with planetary healing.

Shelley Kaehr, Ph.D.

Crystal Skulls Today

Today, there are virtually endless replicas of the crystal skulls fashioned in a wide variety of minerals and stones to suit just about any taste.

As always, when selecting your skull, choose the one that feels best to you and speaks to you at the deepest levels. Remember, it is less about how the skull looks but more about how the skull *feels* to you that will let you know which one is best for you.

Regardless of whether you use your skulls to tap into times past, pray for world peace, or to just to enjoy the beauty of the carving, crystal skulls are what I believe to be an acquired taste. Once you experience it, you will benefit from it for years to come.

"Since in order to speak, one must first listen, learn to speak by listening."

—Rumi

Resources

If this book has piqued your curiosity about these fascinating skulls, here are some resources to check out:

Anna Mitchell-Hedges Official Website:
Want to know more about the Mitchell-Hedges mystery? Anna's site, www.mitchell-hedges.com, has some really neat information, complete with a great photo gallery that includes pictures of her father.

X-Zone Radio host Rob McConnell: My friend Rob has been studying and learning about skulls for decades. He hosts the ever-popular Canadian-based radio program, the X-Zone. Visit Rob online at www.xzone-radio.com.

"That which is false troubles the heart, but truth brings joyous tranquility."

—Rumi

About the Author

Shelley Kaehr, Ph.D. is a lifelong gem enthusiast and researcher who grew up in Albuquerque, NM as the daughter of parents in the mining industry. She is author of over fifteen books, several of which are bestsellers about her passion, gems and minerals. She is also known throughout the world for her groundbreaking work as a hypnotherapist in the field of quantum physics.

Visit Shelley online at
www.shelleykaehr.com

ALSO BY SHELLEY KAEHR, PH.D.

Shelley Kaehr has written over fifteen books on a variety of subjects in the mind-body arena and has recorded dozens of powerful meditation CD's based on her groundbreaking work in the field of regression therapy. Her works include the following:

Lemurian Seeds: Hope for Humanity

Gemstone Enlightenment

Gemstone Journeys

Edgar Cayce's Guide to Gemstones, Minerals, Metals & More

Galactic Healing

Origins of Huna: Secret Behind the Secret Science

Beyond Physical Reality

Explorations Beyond Reality

...and more!

To see a full list of books by Shelley Kaehr, Ph.D., visit www.shelleykaehr.com